Fixed Assets

Register

Table of Contents

Department	Pages

List of Assets

Department: _____

No.	Description of Assets	Qty	Date of Purchase	Make/Brand	Name of Supplier	Value per Piece

List of Assets

Department: _____

No.	Description of Assets	Qty	Date of Purchase	Make/Brand	Name of Supplier	Value per Piece

List of Assets

Department: _____

No.	Description of Assets	Qty	Date of Purchase	Make/Brand	Name of Supplier	Value per Piece

List of Assets

Department: _____

No.	Description of Assets	Qty	Date of Purchase	Make/Brand	Name of Supplier	Value per Piece

List of Assets

Department: _____

No.	Description of Assets	Qty	Date of Purchase	Make/Brand	Name of Supplier	Value per Piece

List of Assets

Department: _____

No.	Description of Assets	Qty	Date of Purchase	Make/Brand	Name of Supplier	Value per Piece

List of Assets

Department: _____

No.	Description of Assets	Qty	Date of Purchase	Make/Brand	Name of Supplier	Value per Piece

List of Assets

Department: _____

No.	Description of Assets	Qty	Date of Purchase	Make/Brand	Name of Supplier	Value per Piece

List of Assets

Department: _____

No.	Description of Assets	Qty	Date of Purchase	Make/Brand	Name of Supplier	Value per Piece

List of Assets

Department: _____

No.	Description of Assets	Qty	Date of Purchase	Make/Brand	Name of Supplier	Value per Piece

List of Assets

Department: _____

No.	Description of Assets	Qty	Date of Purchase	Make/Brand	Name of Supplier	Value per Piece

List of Assets

Department: _____

No.	Description of Assets	Qty	Date of Purchase	Make/Brand	Name of Supplier	Value per Piece

List of Assets

Department: _____

No.	Description of Assets	Qty	Date of Purchase	Make/Brand	Name of Supplier	Value per Piece

List of Assets

Department: _____

No.	Description of Assets	Qty	Date of Purchase	Make/Brand	Name of Supplier	Value per Piece

List of Assets

Department: _____

No.	Description of Assets	Qty	Date of Purchase	Make/Brand	Name of Supplier	Value per Piece

List of Assets

Department: _____

No.	Description of Assets	Qty	Date of Purchase	Make/Brand	Name of Supplier	Value per Piece

List of Assets

Department: _____

No.	Description of Assets	Qty	Date of Purchase	Make/Brand	Name of Supplier	Value per Piece

List of Assets

Department: _____

No.	Description of Assets	Qty	Date of Purchase	Make/Brand	Name of Supplier	Value per Piece

List of Assets

Department: _____

No.	Description of Assets	Qty	Date of Purchase	Make/Brand	Name of Supplier	Value per Piece

List of Assets

Department: _____

No.	Description of Assets	Qty	Date of Purchase	Make/Brand	Name of Supplier	Value per Piece

List of Assets

Department: _____

No.	Description of Assets	Qty	Date of Purchase	Make/Brand	Name of Supplier	Value per Piece

List of Assets

Department: _____

No.	Description of Assets	Qty	Date of Purchase	Make/Brand	Name of Supplier	Value per Piece

List of Assets

Department: _____

No.	Description of Assets	Qty	Date of Purchase	Make/Brand	Name of Supplier	Value per Piece

List of Assets

Department: _____

No.	Description of Assets	Qty	Date of Purchase	Make/Brand	Name of Supplier	Value per Piece

List of Assets

Department: _____

No.	Description of Assets	Qty	Date of Purchase	Make/Brand	Name of Supplier	Value per Piece

List of Assets

Department: _____

No.	Description of Assets	Qty	Date of Purchase	Make/Brand	Name of Supplier	Value per Piece

List of Assets

Department: _____

No.	Description of Assets	Qty	Date of Purchase	Make/Brand	Name of Supplier	Value per Piece

List of Assets

Department: _____

No.	Description of Assets	Qty	Date of Purchase	Make/Brand	Name of Supplier	Value per Piece

List of Assets

Department: _____

No.	Description of Assets	Qty	Date of Purchase	Make/Brand	Name of Supplier	Value per Piece

List of Assets

Department: _____

No.	Description of Assets	Qty	Date of Purchase	Make/Brand	Name of Supplier	Value per Piece

List of Assets

Department: _____

No.	Description of Assets	Qty	Date of Purchase	Make/Brand	Name of Supplier	Value per Piece

List of Assets

Department: _____

No.	Description of Assets	Qty	Date of Purchase	Make/Brand	Name of Supplier	Value per Piece

List of Assets

Department: _____

No.	Description of Assets	Qty	Date of Purchase	Make/Brand	Name of Supplier	Value per Piece

List of Assets

Department: _____

No.	Description of Assets	Qty	Date of Purchase	Make/Brand	Name of Supplier	Value per Piece

List of Assets

Department: _____

No.	Description of Assets	Qty	Date of Purchase	Make/Brand	Name of Supplier	Value per Piece

List of Assets

Department: _____

No.	Description of Assets	Qty	Date of Purchase	Make/Brand	Name of Supplier	Value per Piece

List of Assets

Department: _____

No.	Description of Assets	Qty	Date of Purchase	Make/Brand	Name of Supplier	Value per Piece

List of Assets

Department: _____

No.	Description of Assets	Qty	Date of Purchase	Make/Brand	Name of Supplier	Value per Piece

List of Assets

Department: _____

No.	Description of Assets	Qty	Date of Purchase	Make/Brand	Name of Supplier	Value per Piece

List of Assets

Department: _____

No.	Description of Assets	Qty	Date of Purchase	Make/Brand	Name of Supplier	Value per Piece

List of Assets

Department: _____

No.	Description of Assets	Qty	Date of Purchase	Make/Brand	Name of Supplier	Value per Piece

List of Assets

Department: _____

No.	Description of Assets	Qty	Date of Purchase	Make/Brand	Name of Supplier	Value per Piece

List of Assets

Department: _____

No.	Description of Assets	Qty	Date of Purchase	Make/Brand	Name of Supplier	Value per Piece

List of Assets

Department: _____

No.	Description of Assets	Qty	Date of Purchase	Make/Brand	Name of Supplier	Value per Piece

List of Assets

Department: _____

No.	Description of Assets	Qty	Date of Purchase	Make/Brand	Name of Supplier	Value per Piece

List of Assets

Department: _____

No.	Description of Assets	Qty	Date of Purchase	Make/Brand	Name of Supplier	Value per Piece

List of Assets

Department: _____

No.	Description of Assets	Qty	Date of Purchase	Make/Brand	Name of Supplier	Value per Piece

List of Assets

Department: _____

No.	Description of Assets	Qty	Date of Purchase	Make/Brand	Name of Supplier	Value per Piece

List of Assets

Department: _____

No.	Description of Assets	Qty	Date of Purchase	Make/Brand	Name of Supplier	Value per Piece

List of Assets

Department: _____

No.	Description of Assets	Qty	Date of Purchase	Make/Brand	Name of Supplier	Value per Piece

List of Assets

Department: _____

No.	Description of Assets	Qty	Date of Purchase	Make/Brand	Name of Supplier	Value per Piece

List of Assets

Department: _____

No.	Description of Assets	Qty	Date of Purchase	Make/Brand	Name of Supplier	Value per Piece

List of Assets

Department: _____

No.	Description of Assets	Qty	Date of Purchase	Make/Brand	Name of Supplier	Value per Piece

List of Assets

Department: _____

No.	Description of Assets	Qty	Date of Purchase	Make/Brand	Name of Supplier	Value per Piece

List of Assets

Department: _____

No.	Description of Assets	Qty	Date of Purchase	Make/Brand	Name of Supplier	Value per Piece

List of Assets

Department: _____

No.	Description of Assets	Qty	Date of Purchase	Make/Brand	Name of Supplier	Value per Piece

List of Assets

Department: _____

No.	Description of Assets	Qty	Date of Purchase	Make/Brand	Name of Supplier	Value per Piece

List of Assets

Department: _____

No.	Description of Assets	Qty	Date of Purchase	Make/Brand	Name of Supplier	Value per Piece

List of Assets

Department: _____

No.	Description of Assets	Qty	Date of Purchase	Make/Brand	Name of Supplier	Value per Piece

List of Assets

Department: _____

No.	Description of Assets	Qty	Date of Purchase	Make/Brand	Name of Supplier	Value per Piece

List of Assets

Department: _____

No.	Description of Assets	Qty	Date of Purchase	Make/Brand	Name of Supplier	Value per Piece

List of Assets

Department: _____

No.	Description of Assets	Qty	Date of Purchase	Make/Brand	Name of Supplier	Value per Piece

List of Assets

Department: _____

No.	Description of Assets	Qty	Date of Purchase	Make/Brand	Name of Supplier	Value per Piece

List of Assets

Department: _____

No.	Description of Assets	Qty	Date of Purchase	Make/Brand	Name of Supplier	Value per Piece

List of Assets

Department: _____

No.	Description of Assets	Qty	Date of Purchase	Make/Brand	Name of Supplier	Value per Piece

List of Assets

Department: _____

No.	Description of Assets	Qty	Date of Purchase	Make/Brand	Name of Supplier	Value per Piece

List of Assets

Department: _____

No.	Description of Assets	Qty	Date of Purchase	Make/Brand	Name of Supplier	Value per Piece

List of Assets

Department: _____

No.	Description of Assets	Qty	Date of Purchase	Make/Brand	Name of Supplier	Value per Piece

List of Assets

Department: _____

No.	Description of Assets	Qty	Date of Purchase	Make/Brand	Name of Supplier	Value per Piece

List of Assets

Department: _____

No.	Description of Assets	Qty	Date of Purchase	Make/Brand	Name of Supplier	Value per Piece

List of Assets

Department: _____

No.	Description of Assets	Qty	Date of Purchase	Make/Brand	Name of Supplier	Value per Piece

List of Assets

Department: _____

No.	Description of Assets	Qty	Date of Purchase	Make/Brand	Name of Supplier	Value per Piece

List of Assets

Department: _____

No.	Description of Assets	Qty	Date of Purchase	Make/Brand	Name of Supplier	Value per Piece

List of Assets

Department: _____

No.	Description of Assets	Qty	Date of Purchase	Make/Brand	Name of Supplier	Value per Piece

List of Assets

Department: _____

No.	Description of Assets	Qty	Date of Purchase	Make/Brand	Name of Supplier	Value per Piece

List of Assets

Department: _____

No.	Description of Assets	Qty	Date of Purchase	Make/Brand	Name of Supplier	Value per Piece

List of Assets

Department: _____

No.	Description of Assets	Qty	Date of Purchase	Make/Brand	Name of Supplier	Value per Piece

List of Assets

Department: _____

No.	Description of Assets	Qty	Date of Purchase	Make/Brand	Name of Supplier	Value per Piece

List of Assets

Department: _____

No.	Description of Assets	Qty	Date of Purchase	Make/Brand	Name of Supplier	Value per Piece

List of Assets

Department: _____

No.	Description of Assets	Qty	Date of Purchase	Make/Brand	Name of Supplier	Value per Piece

List of Assets

Department: _____

No.	Description of Assets	Qty	Date of Purchase	Make/Brand	Name of Supplier	Value per Piece

List of Assets

Department: _____

No.	Description of Assets	Qty	Date of Purchase	Make/Brand	Name of Supplier	Value per Piece

List of Assets

Department: _____

No.	Description of Assets	Qty	Date of Purchase	Make/Brand	Name of Supplier	Value per Piece

List of Assets

Department: _____

No.	Description of Assets	Qty	Date of Purchase	Make/Brand	Name of Supplier	Value per Piece

List of Assets

Department: _____

No.	Description of Assets	Qty	Date of Purchase	Make/Brand	Name of Supplier	Value per Piece

List of Assets

Department: _____

No.	Description of Assets	Qty	Date of Purchase	Make/Brand	Name of Supplier	Value per Piece

List of Assets

Department: _____

No.	Description of Assets	Qty	Date of Purchase	Make/Brand	Name of Supplier	Value per Piece

List of Assets

Department: _____

No.	Description of Assets	Qty	Date of Purchase	Make/Brand	Name of Supplier	Value per Piece

List of Assets

Department: _____

No.	Description of Assets	Qty	Date of Purchase	Make/Brand	Name of Supplier	Value per Piece

List of Assets

Department: _____

No.	Description of Assets	Qty	Date of Purchase	Make/Brand	Name of Supplier	Value per Piece

List of Assets

Department: _____

No.	Description of Assets	Qty	Date of Purchase	Make/Brand	Name of Supplier	Value per Piece

List of Assets

Department: _____

No.	Description of Assets	Qty	Date of Purchase	Make/Brand	Name of Supplier	Value per Piece

List of Assets

Department: _____

No.	Description of Assets	Qty	Date of Purchase	Make/Brand	Name of Supplier	Value per Piece

List of Assets

Department: _____

No.	Description of Assets	Qty	Date of Purchase	Make/Brand	Name of Supplier	Value per Piece

List of Assets

Department: _____

No.	Description of Assets	Qty	Date of Purchase	Make/Brand	Name of Supplier	Value per Piece

List of Assets

Department: _____

No.	Description of Assets	Qty	Date of Purchase	Make/Brand	Name of Supplier	Value per Piece

List of Assets

Department: _____

No.	Description of Assets	Qty	Date of Purchase	Make/Brand	Name of Supplier	Value per Piece

List of Assets

Department: _____

No.	Description of Assets	Qty	Date of Purchase	Make/Brand	Name of Supplier	Value per Piece

List of Assets

Department: _____

No.	Description of Assets	Qty	Date of Purchase	Make/Brand	Name of Supplier	Value per Piece